RETURNING YOUR CALL

PRINCETON SERIES OF
CONTEMPORARY POETS

Returning Your Call

POEMS

BY LEONARD NATHAN

PRINCETON UNIVERSITY PRESS

Copyright © 1975 by Princeton University Press
Published by Princeton University Press, Princeton and London
All Rights Reserved

Library of Congress Cataloging in Publication Data will
be found on the last printed page of this book

Publication of this book has been aided by the Louis A. Robb
Fund of Princeton University Press

This book has been composed in Linotype Times Roman

Printed in the United States of America
by Princeton University Press, Princeton, New Jersey

For Carol

ACKNOWLEDGMENTS

The poems "Hay Fever" and "Letter" appeared originally in *The New Yorker*. The following poems have also appeared previously: "Memo," "Powers" (in "Four for the Queen of Sheba"), and "Stonecutter's Holiday" in *Antæus*; "Invitation" in *Antioch Review*; "Division of Labor" in *Chelsea*; "Inside" and "Niagara" in *Chicago Tribune*; "The Sacrifice" in *Choice Magazine*; "Greetings" (in "Four for the Queen of Sheba") and "Washing Socks" in *Counter/Measures*; "The Attendant," "Pillow Book Song," "Pumpernickel," "Sixtieth Annual Ethnological Survey," and "Slippers" in *Epoch*; "Short Pastoral" in *Mark in Time: Portraits & Poetry*, Glide Publications; "The Mouths" (as "These Are") in *Malahat Review*; "Audit" in *Minnesota Review*; "The Penance" and "Sorry" in *New Republic*; "The Gardens," "He," "Honorable Mention," and "Trying" in *New York Times*; "Averaging Out" and "Trees" in *Northwest Review*; "Four Position Papers" (from "Eight Position Papers"), "One for Beauty," and "One for the Poet" in *Perspective*; "Poem for Late in the Year" (as "Autumn Poem"), "Retirement Party," and "Wires" in *Prairie Schooner*; "Confession," "From the Cold Outside," "Revival Meeting for Wheel Chairs and Stretchers," and "To the City" in *Quarterly Review of Literature*; "Great" in *Seneca Review*; "Breathing Exercises," "Good Morning Song," "Jane Seagrim's Party," and "Judgment" in *Shenandoah*; "Foretellings" in *Tennessee Poetry Journal*. Some of these poems appeared in slightly different form.

CONTENTS

I. REFLECTIONS OF A LEFT-HANDED MIRROR TWIN

Breathing Exercises 3
Good-Morning Song 6
Memo 7
Poem for Late in the Year 8
Portrait of the Artist in His Forties 9
One for Beauty 10
One for the Poet 12
Muse, My Revolutionary 14
Slippers 15
Letter 16

II. DUETS FOR ONE LOVING VOICE

The Mouths 19
Averaging Out 21
Niagara 22
Sorry 23
Confession 24
From the Cold Outside 25
Inside 26
Pillow Book Song 27
Washing Socks 28
Judgment 29
The Gardens 30
Wires 31

III. INTERVIEWS WITH THE LOSING SIDE

Pumpernickel 35
Jane Seagrim's Party 36
Captain Darnell 37
Four for the Queen of Sheba 38
Revival Meeting for Wheel Chairs and Stretchers 42
Invitation 43
He 44
Foretellings 45
The Attendant 47
Great 48

CONTENTS

IV. MINORITY REPORTS

The Sacrifice	51
Four Position Papers	53
The Invention	54
The Final Conviction of Pompey Blackman	56
Booker T. Washington in Heaven	57
Cleaning Lady	58
Division of Labor	60
Sixtieth Annual Ethnological Survey	61
The Penance	62

V. A FEW OCCASIONS TO CELEBRATE

Stonecutter's Holiday	65
Retirement Party	66
Trying	67
Hay Fever	68
Honorable Mention	69
Short Pastoral	70
Skins	71
To the City	72
Trees	74
The Guru	75
Audit	76

I
REFLECTIONS OF A LEFT-HANDED MIRROR TWIN

BREATHING EXERCISES

My mother phoning from far off:
How are you? How are you really? Really?

A long dumbness fills with breathing.
How much does she want to know? Really?

I'm fine, fighting, making passes,
Doing my job. Does that sound right?

No, it sounds as if somebody bugged
The phone and I'm talking for the bugger.

Which reminds me: I'm Leonard Nathan whose grandpa
Changed his last name—too Jewish.

I'm not Leonard Nathan. I'm hiding
Down here and have fooled the psychiatrists.

You know what I do? I breathe slyly.
It's nice to breathe, that's the spirit.

Wonderful. Inside Leonard
Nathan is a little spirit.

Rocks in the desert also breathe—
More spirits, and water breathes deep.

If somebody screws your mouth shut, whistle
Through your nose. For God's sake, keep breathing.

Inhale fifteen seconds, thinking
OM, hold ten, exhale fifteen.

Grandpa scares me holding his breath.
His last address was an oxygen tent.

My belly rises and falls, tidal,
But the phone ringing can freeze me solid.

Hello, this is a rock calling
From the floor of the sea, your great grandma.

Hello, this is an empty bottle
Calling from the desert: I'm going crazy.

Put father on. He's watching the Jets
Blow somebody right out of the stadium.

He breathes deep in himself, precious
To himself. Daddy's a real rock.

My son is inhaling a whole sky
Of filth. He hates telephones and ideas.

I ask, are you there? Mere breathing
Answers. That also scares me.

Listen, I'll breathe with you, inhale
For grandpa, exhale for a grandchild unborn.

Sometimes I get the cadence of things
And breathe with them, like music, but not.

They paraphrased Hsieh Ho: "The life
Of the spirit in the rhythm of things." Nope.

You can't paraphrase. You can't say anything.
You live in a tent deep under water.

And someone has just stopped breathing again.
Grandpa, names change nothing but words!

This is a prayer to your absence. Hear me.
I lean close. I hiss. I breathe into you.

Out of the stupid air of the desert
I made it and the musculature of the sea.

It is so much wind, but I want it back,
Sucking it out of your life, my spirit.

My mother won't hear. She listens far off
To her self. That's how I am really.

GOOD-MORNING SONG

Miss America, this here
Is your beautiful friend,
The middle-aged poet, dumped off the back end
Of sleep for pigs to root in.

The same. That natty chaunting spirit
Reciting last night by candles te tum te tum,
Making love seem so many good words,
Sex wiser than Plato.

You also were something else—
Soft and sensitive light,
A bounty of lights embodied and bathed,
Saying yes and yes O yes.

Don't be sad. It's the spirit
That leads us on. Consult your TV,
Refrigerator, your own biddable heart
Or sweet lavender toilet.

MEMO

He did it, my left-handed mirror twin
With his heart on the wrong side
And his far-off look.
I never left this office.

You can hear him now—over the wine
Making his promises, his eyes
Getting greener by candle flicker
And watery music.

We were seventeen when I said:
You stay here if you want, I'm going to grow up
And be a serious wage earner. He spat
Like a movie cowpoke.

Now he's playing Charles Boyer.
Sure he loves you. That's all he's good for, loving,
So forget him. Love is too simple
For this world.

POEM FOR LATE IN
THE YEAR

It is harder now to be someone else.
The smooth masks of Juan,
Of Odysseus, mouth open for a brave lie,
Hang on the wall now, masks.

What is said to women has lost
Its silken under-meaning, its rendezvous
Of silence beyond itself, yes
The mere opposite of mere no.

It is hard enough to be one's self:
What is this at the center
That answers like a dog to a given name?
Old habit, a chronic face in the mirror.

PORTRAIT OF THE ARTIST IN HIS FORTIES

That look is coming from so far away, the glass
Of red, the wedge of cheese before him seem waiting
Meekly. Under his fingers, a knife is glowing
    Like a neglected power.

Figures like people keep flowing together to say
A thing unheard of—he leans to catch it. Nonsense.
Five smoky days of rain and everything whispers
    Or taps to be noticed.

The face is a blind man's face that, talked to, cocks,
Wanting this once to get the story right,
But won't. A wife may complain, three children cry,
    But a flute contains them.

The talk is of time and money, how rain has found
A leak in the roof. Meanwhile, the sole survivor
Wades toward a painted beach, deafened by birds,
    Blinded by water.

ONE FOR BEAUTY

I tell Beauty, at Her most loving, to shut up.
I can't praise Her in all this racket.

Any one of nine sirens could be
For me, ME, and She wants praise.

I say: Look at the front page, you nitwit.
Life is too serious for this clowning.

She thinks She's Mae West, or Sophia Loren
Whispering *Caro, caro mio.*

Or Indira Gandhi cooling two hundred
And fifty million hot males.

Someday I'll tell Her it's not loving
She wants, but attention, all the attention.

The bread of the world can burn if only
We treat Her right. She thinks we need Her.

We. The men. She doesn't think much of women,
The silly bitches. They bore Her. She's cracked.

Or so innocent She thinks the assassin
Has Her in mind when he aims. What's death?

She thinks the hard-hats dream of Her swathed
In the flag. What's race or class or money?

She thinks the poets do it for Her
Out of reverence, and soldiers too for Her glory.

As to those other bitches, Justice
And Truth, they are cold and ugly. Who cares?

I tell Her: Here are two pills. For godsake,
Sleep. It's time for the last news.

In Miami fifty girls parade measurements by
For a crown. Beauty thinks that's great.

She thinks we can send home
The UN now that we've got Miss World.

I say it's vulgar. She laughs. I say there's something
Inhuman about it. She says sure.

And yawns and tells me: Get with your time,
And stretches and says: What lasts is style.

And now suddenly She wants to dance.
Where is Your social conscience, You whore?

I whisper this in Her ear as we dance.

ONE FOR THE POET

Hey (I shouted), you well-kept Establishment type!
Before you go up to get your honor, answer
Me this. (The cops began shoving us back about here.)

What do you do for a living? A college pays you!
Isn't that nice. Did Blake teach college, or Whitman?
(Now the crowd began to shout Whitman, Whitman!

And the cops, who like stricter lines than Whitman, began
Shoving harder, bringing their sticks up under our chins.)
Was Keats a professor? Does Pound have a Ph.D.?

I bet you compose on a big mahogany desk,
Warm in the winter, cool in the summer, a garden
Outside, safe in a riot, dreaming of honor.

I bet you think that under that rich blue blazer
You're François Villon or Thomas and someday you'll tear off
The blazer and show us a hot Spanish heart, a Lorca.

(The cops were putting their gas masks on and I thought:
My God, for poetry they do it! It's really important.
And the crowd was chanting, defiant, Neruda and Williams.)

Hey (I screamed) before they give you your honor,
Think of your folks who were lucky to get into high school,
To get a job in Depression, to eat, to live.

The poet turned to me then while the crowd was howling
Ginsberg and Snyder, and held my eyes in his eyes,
I who never published or no one had heard of.

He held my eyes as the crowd wailed foreign names
Or nonsense like names with a future and the cops were loading
Their weapons by order and scanning their lines for order.

He held my eyes in his eyes till I felt I was inside
His seeing, I who out of my cellar was lost,
Was naked, was honest only because I was nothing,

I who walked up the stairs to his honor while the crowd
Lamented the brutal absence of poetry, though the cops
With regular ranks finally contained them in silence,

I who accepted his honor, ate of his banquet,
Spoke his right words and left with his honor, fearing
That someone would know me and sting me back to my cellar.

It waits for me still to be honest, to come back with nothing.

MUSE, MY REVOLUTIONARY

                    You come to me
On ball bearings out of Detroit,
The down stroke of steel punches thumping
Like rim shots every time you put
Your foot down.
                    You come bearing
The five-hundred-thousandth copy
Of *Revolution in April* and I accept you
Like all the by-products of this System,
Like a swan swimming out of oily steam
Or a bar of soap or love mislabeled
On the bottom shelf of the supermarket
Or the book you bear denying the System.

You say you came first from the village of April
Whose wet edible grass no anthropologist
Has yet trampled, whose children rule
Under green light thatched over them
By adoring palms.
                    I love you for your lies
Also and for that rebellious sweetness
Which is a dysfunction of the System
That nevertheless made you up
To specification. That you don't work
Is a wonder, a triumph of the System singing
In its gears of breakdown, of accidental grass,
Of another chance to create the impossible
To specification.
                    Now, April,
My revolution, tell me your plan.

SLIPPERS

These old slippers are lined with wool,
A kettle trills, a furnace purrs below
The carpet; another mug of imported coffee.

Radio, trill me Mozart, purr me
Brahms. Asia? I don't want Asia.
For God's sake, keep Asia quiet!

I sent a surplus rifle over
To pacify Asia, and you say Ho
In the bathroom, Mao in the bedroom.

But this is my parlor. The rest is Asia's
If Asia wants it. Ho for waste,
Mao for nightmare, Mozart for slippers.

I could, if I had to, fit in one slipper.

LETTER

I'm writing this to you
From two miles inside a Chinese painting
Called "Mountains After Rain."

For a long time I too dreamed of money
In the pockets of love dining nightly
On power and Peking Duck.

I was called intimate first names
In silken rooms, and in public deferred to
As "The Master."

Exiled, I thought: "This is the end
Of the world," and it was, a narrow trail
Westering into the fog.

The painter wanted that intense green
Of autumn just before the world
Renounces itself.

This then is not death or happiness
But a long comfortable meditation
On the impossible.

So I write to prepare you for the next disappointment,
Its beauty, its loving art, and its need,
And for the disappointment after.

II
DUETS FOR ONE
LOVING VOICE

THE MOUTHS

These are mouths. They contain
Everything: hers and mine together.
It's perfectly dark in here
Even at noon, at the very center,
Past boredom, past
The slow river of misery, past
Even pleasure, past all
But touching the whole length
Of this earth. I end
Where she begins—where?
Wherever we can't feel anymore—
Nowhere. In Nampur someone is mourning;
We will make good that loss. In Koshu
A child comes too soon. We keep it
Alive by our warmth. A fox,
This once in all the world, loosens
Its jaws, appeased, and the chicken
Flaps up. All begging is done with,
All injustice, for all is given
And there's plenty to give: fingers,
Hips, cheeks, tongues, hair.

But when we come apart, helpless
To hold together, we know already
In a few hours alone
We can be overrun by want
And nothing can satisfy us
Though our mouths open to protest
Or only to gasp.

Beside myself with her,
There is this other separate love
Reaching silent over for pity,
Stroking, useless, her face
As if she too were hungry,
Sick, foreign, unloved.

AVERAGING OUT

You are so young you think
I'm speaking in my own voice
When it's really a faucet speaking
To say: The pressure's too much;
Or the stuffing of your sofa
Sighing: What's inside comes out
So sadly; or the garbage man
Humming blues as he hauls away
Chicken bones and empty cans;
Or the Lord of Kicks bitching
Over how little humans offer Him.

You think you know how average
It always is, how temporary
It always was, how it's maybe
Getting worse, but that girls are tough.

Someday I'm going to speak
In my own voice, and tell you
How close we are. You'll have to cover
My mouth with your free hand—
That's how close. You don't know
Any more about it than I do.
No one does; no one wants to.

NIAGARA

Looking into the Falls, I heard it sing:
Marriage, marriage, one life always,
Beginning to end in simple water music.
And I thought, by you, this isn't music for men,
Who are always bespoken in two places at once,
Who partially stand in the middle of great music
Distracted by distance. I put myself in this poem
With you and with marrying waters, and look at me—still
A little apart, wishing for one whole life
But singing this far-off solo right
In the face of the music, as though it could solve me.

SORRY

After the fifth beer,
Milwaukee softens, fine snow
Wafting me back to the hotel
Where the warmth of the lobby
Floats me up to my room.

I'm calling long distance now
To say: It's all right, love, after all.
But am told the number has changed,
Sorry, unlisted—
Well, that sobers Milwaukee.

The window looks darkly out on stone,
And I've found another place to lose touch with.
Tomorrow in Boston, I'll call myself here
And they'll just have to say:
He's gone.

CONFESSION

All right then—I am Napoleon
And you, you've got to be Joan of Arc.

I've just fallen back through a winter of ice,
Done in by a sublime vision of one world.

And you've come home from a hard day of torture,
Dragging chains, still defying the Establishment.

Now you understand my rotten mood and I
Can appreciate your haggard, put-upon look.

And they think our miseries are commonplace miseries,
That we bought them from a marriage counselor second hand!

You go on pressing your palms to that heaving breast,
I'll just stand here gazing out over the world.

FROM THE COLD OUTSIDE

(After Ronsard, much after)

Forty years from now it's night—suddenly
The knitting needles sink and you stare
Into the fire's heart and mutter
Lines I wrote for you once, crying:
"My God! That's how Leonard praised me
When I was lovely and pretended not to care."

The cleaning woman will viciously tilt
Her bored head and, knowing our history,
Think: "She was a lucky bitch
To have that man put her in songs. Look at her
Now: two-thirds dead, buried
Under shawls and sweaters."

I'll be elsewhere then: shy bones
Tickled by roots, and you disgusted
With that virgin pose assumed when there seemed
A time for every whim. Look at you now.
A rose must live to live. Tomorrow—nothing
Or a cold colder than yours.

INSIDE

This is the inside, love,
This light room, your hip curving
Into me, my hand exactly
Suited to yours, all under
The covers, like one warm life.

Outside, it's raining, dark,
And someone, to whom this town is foreign,
Crosses a street against
The hard shine of headlights;
Water drops off the brim of his hat,
His socks are sodden
And no one waits for him.

Suddenly I'm cold,
Right in the core of the spine
Where it all began,
A blind wriggling through water
Toward what?
This cold is the doctor's examining room,
Naked, and has no remedy.

You fit me
As if always intended to.
I wish that were proof.

PILLOW BOOK SONG

The Lady Izumi
Shikibu,
A fragrant blur
In this wavering dream
Of sleeves, bent
Her moon face
Closer, till I
Assumed a love
As soft and subtle
As mist, but she
Said flatly: "It's time
To give me your life,"
And that seemed so ancient
A habit here
That I was about
To say yes, yes,
When simple moonlight
Saved me, opening
My eyes, sitting
Me up, sodden-
Headed, belly
Packed with ice,
Mouth poisoned,
And so bitterly
I said at the moon:
"I don't know
Any Lady
Shikibu."

WASHING SOCKS

Penelope, old dear, you write
That all that keeps you sane these days
Is washing socks, faded socks,
And add: "For godsake, come on home!"

I'm out here having adventures, sleeping
With goddesses, though sometimes I feel
Like a swine. I'm battling giant man-
Eating abstractions. I'm at sea.

There was the Island of Romance, the greener
Islands of Marx, of Freud, the misty
Isle of Zen and the volcanic Sartre.
And then there is plain old Ithaca.

You're bending over the tub, hearing
The kids bicker in the background, thinking
Of all the passes you passed up,
All for the owner of these faded socks.

And I will get there soon. War
Takes a long time, abstractions centuries
To escape, romance to wake from, and the sea
Itself is no friend to marriage.

I will come up the beach barefoot,
Grinning, and you'll make me sit right there
And put on those socks, smiling bitterly
Down because they no longer fit.

But for the kids, make the best of it.

JUDGMENT

When my women (you can count them off
On one hand) foregather in Heaven to judge
And make me a Hell, unstitching my life
And holding the pieces up for a laugh
Among friends, O, I will be staring down
At my feet like a country boy and be grateful,
For what if they turned their backs or forgot
How once I troubled them? Dozens of poems,
A million unpublished words, and countless
Caressing silences—all for a little
Attention. I'll stand there stark as new snow
To their gaze, loving the consummate way
They undid me so fatally down to the truth
Which set out ages ago toward their praise.

THE GARDENS

(*For M.R.*)

She, among rosy changes,
Flaring reds and whites
Exploding at her side, dying
In her arms, looks over at him
Who can sit all day
Before one dwarf pine,
Fixed in spare gravel,
Merely breathing.

She for ripeness, acting
Through death, was made, he
For persistence with no claims
But a little green in winter.

Love, an afterthought, has grafted
On his pine no roses, nor added
One more day to her annuals,
And, so it seems, is only human,
Changing with them, persisting
For them alone.

WIRES

So we can be loving still,
Our leaders talk fast on red telephones
Thinning to copper wires
Drawn through the ice of Moscow,
Or they bounce in long waves off tiny stations
In space, listening intent to earphones
Translate the remote into familiar garble,
And glance now and then at themselves
On TV instantly picturing
The far-away face of crisis.

Sometimes my hand takes hours
To get through the wires of her hair
Because I'm sending a message by them
To all the tiny stations around
So we can be loving still: Keep
In touch, keep
In touch.

III
INTERVIEWS WITH THE
LOSING SIDE

PUMPERNICKEL

Feh! You call this pumpernickel,
This a political system, a living?
What do you call this? Forty years
Uncle Morris has been dreaming Russia.

The comrades there, snow on their whiskers, rub
Red hands by the hearth, its fire kindling their eyes
As they praise heroes, toast revolution,
Sing love songs in tears, untranslatable.

Of late though, Uncle Morris is dreaming
Badly and considers a flight of fancy
To Israel. But its absence of snow chills him.
What do you do with a camel, an Arab?

So he waits his exile out like an unused alias
Of Trotsky, rocking a chair designed
In Ohio, watching the Fords go by
As he chews slowly like a man cursing.

JANE SEAGRIM'S PARTY

This calls for a toast. She hates
To admit it, but Jane is one hundred today
And reporters are coming by to watch
Her blow the candles out and ask,
Dearie, how, how did you do it
And how can we, who love speed,
Drink, cigars and have so deep
A sense of the tragic? And she will grin,
Exposing blackness on either side
Of her original stumpy canines and maybe
Wink who laid out three good husbands,
Receives post cards from her kids' kids
Having fun in another world
With people in it, can't even follow
TV to see the good life
In color—like two weeks in Hawaii—
She's missed, and is terrified of children
Who want, hugging, to break her bones,
Eats mush and drinks tea, thank you,
Won't be sampling her own cake,
And anyway the taste buds have all bloomed
And died long ago and it's shocking
To sit on the toilet and look down.

Nevertheless, one joy is left—
To pull, if she had it, from under her skirts,
A dainty pistol out and, right
In the middle of their disbelief,
Shoot these smartasses dead
Who thought this old life
Had no more to show them.

CAPTAIN DARNELL

Fifty years walking on water
And now, safe in port, he could hear
Every two A.M. the tide chanting:
"Darnell, Darnell," its dark mouth
So fluent, one kiss would leave only
His hat floating, and he whispered: "No,
No," sick that his heart was still
Beaten by desire.
      It was like standing
Up to his waist in the tide of sleep, feeling
Its wanton muscular pull, his name
Sung by the black waters beyond.
So he who had steered, he thought, his whole life
Toward dry haven, was stranded here alone,
His ankles braided by seaweed to a deeper
Thing.
  And his groan roused his old wife
Who muttered into his back: "It's only a dream,
Darnell. Go back to sleep."
         So, tired of standing,
He lay back down in the solvent cradle,
Sensing the salt in his blood lift
And fall with the salt of the sea, his name
Becoming merely the sound the water makes
As it shapes the drift.
       This time he wished
He would wake again, after so many lives
And havens, satisfied as water.

FOUR FOR
THE QUEEN OF SHEBA

I. Greetings

When my grandpa got off steerage
Smelling of Russia, yours was beating
His hoe into the hot dust
Of Tennessee for peanuts.

The coaches that hauled our lives west
Erode on forgotten sidings and neither of us
Knows what broke our great grandmothers' hearts—
Pogrom, slavery, unspeakable love.

So nothing separates us now
But our own strangeness, a man who looks down
Embarrassed at his pale hands, a woman
Who stares warily out of her darkness.

Hello, my fellow American.

II. Powers

You admit that Grandma said, putting
You on the train north: be a good girl,
Be still, be who you are. But you decided
To be some sort of queen instead.

There are precincts even in Chicago that loving
Can win and so you loved strongly,
Parted hard, and stood at the far end
Of the room awaiting the next introduction.

One day Grandma became Mississippi,
Worn-out earth, and no one was left to judge
Your power. They deferred to or fought it, as they dared,
But you grew stronger every loving year.

If now, noblesse oblige, you took
The same train backward to Mississippi,
There'd be Grandma waving slowly up
At a small face, then stepping slowly back,

Bitterly satisfied with her emissary.

III. The Inheritance

Don't I hear in your voice
The pipers of Kush, the talking drums
Of the Yoruba, the Mississippi flowing
Through summer nights, a dawn solo
At the Terrace Club? O, I do not.

I hear Grandma rustling stiffly
Around the dark house, a limp dishrag
In her hand. She breathes hard, but refuses
To moan, though your life has buried hers.
Breathing was all she had left to pass on.

And now you waste her with a sigh.

IV. The Door

In the room of your first loneliness,
Crowded with sleepers, you dreamed of the man
At the door sent away by Grandma,
Who avoided your eyes the rest of that day.
You dreamed it was probably your lost father.

He went off alone again
Into the red dust of Tennessee,
And Grandma followed him and later
Your mother. There was nothing for it
But to be proud and watchful.

People keep on opening that old door
But not seeing you and besides
You moved on up to Chicago and got
So beautiful you could send anyone
Away and still have friends.

·But someone is going to ease in one night,
Lean over the bed, and say:
"It's all right now" and the room will—whoosh—
Light up like a surprise party where you'll see
Everything you ever wanted through your tears.

REVIVAL MEETING FOR WHEEL CHAIRS AND STRETCHERS

Don't tell him about the beauty of losing
Or about miracles. He has had bread
Turn to stone in his bowels, sewage
Back up to his eyes, his life wither out
From under him, except the pain.

Down from the hills, across the flatlands
He jerked and snorted, hauling into L.A.
Under a black sky through hostile traffic
And squatted, hearing on the radio Great Ideas
That would save him and didn't, so he spat and glared back.

Tell him instead of a free trip to the Hawaiian Hilton,
A tenth floor suite, meals served under silver
By small and selfless men, roses changed
Every day, a color TV, Jack Daniels,
And a girl who would do it for nothing but fun.

He would rise from the stretcher like pure spirit
Singing hallelujah, converted to a faith
You could hardly tell from indifference, a life
That never had to come down to the world again
Where the sick and the poor fight, crouching, over the dirt.

Meanwhile the sky gets blacker under his nails
And the prayers for salvation flame in his ears
Like curses. He has come all this way
To be saved and there's talk of sin, of cause
And effect, but he knows he's dying by sheer miracle.

INVITATION

We asked the assassin to dinner,
Believing a feast of reasons
Would bring him loving to justice,
But then he looked up with the whites
Of his eyes and softly inquired:
Who provided this meat?
And down the long barrel of silence,
Every knife there glittered.

HE

He's coming. I saw him last night in a dream,
Hiking the edge of a dusty road
Heading west. Take a good look at your Whitman,
Then tuck it between the Bible and Life,
For he's coming with two days' growth of beard
On his thin face, a book of Zen
In his sack, and also Camus and others
More recent you may have only heard of.
He's finished with school and done with poems
And novels, done with pot and with sex,
With cycles, with tattooed portraits of Hitler;
Now he's seeking a red brick wall,
A man in a blindfold standing before it,
Himself; so here he comes and he won't
Be our salesman or bum either; no—
He's entering politics. He counts on our dreams
To put him in, and the wall to support him.

FORETELLINGS

I. *Fox*
The egg is splitting. A moist bill peeps through.
That barn is in my nose, that hay, that nest,
That egg, and also, in the litter under the porch,
One among seven blind black fur balls.
I sniff the whole thing out far off, a meeting
Which ends with a bad smell I will not smell,
And trot forward, though the hair on my back crawls.

II. *Inspector*
In the disadvantaged house that people keep leaving
A son is born with a bomb in his left hand,
Enemy of my life, a helpless child
I cannot touch. He lies there plotting my life.

III. *Spider*
In the warm paralyzing hum
Of the wasp factory, a pair of wings,
Among a hundred pairs of wings,
Dries and stretches. A sting zeroes in.
My back, feeling it come
Through the tender air, contracts, goes numb.

IV. *Captain*
In the foreign colonel's house, a son is born
With a map in his palm. When I am an old general,
He'll meet me, and thoroughly planned, defeat me.
His new tactics will turn my old ones aside.
I'll stare at nothing then, as he does now.

V. *Father*
My son is born with a different look in his eyes.
His very first step will be away from me
And he'll keep on walking though I call out to warn
That when he gets wherever he wants to be,
He'll also support a son who will walk away.
And then we'll both know—a long line of sons
Walking in willful directions out of our hands,
Sometimes turning their heads to gauge their progress.
Then he and I will be allies against sons.

THE ATTENDANT

Before everything goes under
And after the last rescue team turns home,
Having left its ensign lost in the snow,
Someone attends to the world.

Someone always attends—
Old gloves and bent trowel, the gardener
Whose wife thinks he's crazy and says so
To anyone who'll listen.

When sun became rain became ice,
He stayed out there nursing alone
A little green while we sipped hot chocolate by the fire,
Bitching or kidding around.

We asked him if he thought he was Francis
Of the Pines or Admiral Perry. He answered shyly
Something about roses. Roses! We turned away
And flirted with his young wife.

GREAT

It's great to be miserable and know it—
Pascal. That's manhood: misery.
It's great. My dog Oliver
Is not great, nor the apple tree.

Pity them, lacking this aptitude
For being great like you and me,
Or my father who is even greater,
More prone to misery.

His ulcer tells him at three AM:
You are great, Jack, and his spine,
When he pulls on a sock, measures his greatness
In miles of glorifying pain.

Sometimes I catch in Oliver's eyes
A shade of something very like grief,
But no—my own reflection; and the apple?
How can it hurt to lose a leaf?

Let's get together and compare miseries;
It will be great, because whoever
Has most we'll give a prize—Pascal's
Jawbone or a day in the skull of Oliver.

IV
MINORITY REPORTS

THE SACRIFICE

One life for jetting back
To Chicago, one for the Greyhound bus
To Memphis, three to wring a little green
From Tennessee dirt, one to stumble
Behind pack mules half delirious
To Carolina, finally one
To board the slave ship bound for the Gold Coast
Where at last we stride through foam under torches
Toward the shut shore to find there
Someone who looks like you, stripped,
Wrists tied to her belly, staring out
Over the senseless black waters,
The other girls sobbing or moaning.

I want to tell her that seven lives
And love will make up for all this
And that I need her forgiveness now,
But am so implicated, the slavers
Begin to treat me as equal.
                        Besides
She's wholly absorbed in the endless heave
And collapse, heave and collapse of the sea,
Taking in as her own its blackness
And misery, letting its monotonous thunder
Be a curse to drown out human curses.

And here you say, smiling even,
That nothing helps, not seventy lives

Or the binding gifts of guilt, and that love
Can only forgive the near and human
And that she went beyond the human,
Wife of the waters, unbearable mother.

FOUR POSITION PAPERS

---

1. I look down at my hands amazed:
   They are white with inexperience,
   And open as if they expected
   A present for being open.

2. It is like finding a hand without its body,
   And knowing the body is not far off. Who wants to find it?
   The assassin, on the shoulders of his people,
   Shouts: Here I am! Who wants to find him?

3. One shoe is Viet Nam. It is full of blood.
   The other is a sneaker found in a riot
   Still knotted. They fit, but don't match;
   Left strides me hard to my killer, right to my victim.

4. She is black and lovely who shut my mouth
   With a look, for under man and woman,
   Under pigment, there is human.
   Who taught human to hate us too?

THE INVENTION

When Eli Whitney dreamed up the cotton gin
It snowed whiteness over all
The Deep South, and over dark skins
One, two, three chalky layers,
So the plantation owners sang hymns
While the slaves stood blinded
In the candescent fields,
Only their faces, hands, and feet protesting
That darkness was not yet
To be wholly hidden.

But the spinners of England spun,
Shift after shift under the coal smoke,
To whiten the whole world,
Shipping millions of pale gowns
Like an army of spirits
Up the Congo, where elephants paused,
Patient as fog-colored hills,
While progress dwindled
Like puffs of smoke
Into the black interior.

Then it began to drizzle fine ash
From Savannah to Manchester dimming
The radiance of all fresh linen,
Graying the heads of missionaries who sit

By the river and weep faded tears
As in an obscure dream of Eli Whitney
When he wakes just as he's ripped
Into the dark below
By his own spiked invention
And, O Boss, it won't wash.

THE FINAL CONVICTION OF POMPEY BLACKMAN

While they transacted millions in a heaven
Of high finance, they could hear Pompey Blackman
Whisper up through the vents from the basement furnace,
"Black midnight is my cry.
Black midnight is my cry."
But they imagined it was the heating system
Humming up seventy storeys for their comfort.

While they were playing love on their secretaries
After a seized day of many good fortunes,
They could hear Pomp down there muttering,
"This rock is burning too.
There's no hiding place in the rock."
But they thought that maybe something was stuck
In the throat of a pipe so they rattled on.

But while they were pounding on the hot warped doors
And smoke coiled over their blistered shoes,
All they could hear was their own howling
And the groans of roasting girders, as Pomp,
His black face blazing with revelation
And police flashlights, shouted over and over,
"When you lynched your own sweet Jesus,
He didn't say a word, not a mumbalin' word."

BOOKER T. WASHINGTON IN HEAVEN

When Booker T. Washington came lowly
To Heaven, angels drew back
Wary. Was, under four layers
Of creamy forgiveness, Nat Turner hunkering
In the compressed sweat of his outrage,
Or would Washington, snowing the Lord,
Bring the Southern skies under a starry
Tuskegee and certain darker angels
Be brought up from below to learn useful crafts
And smile humbly?

Those same wary seraphim would gladly embrace
Malcolm X whose sword flared
With the same simple fire as theirs—
Supernatural indignation. So when Booker T.
Came from the Lord's mansion and said only
That he was satisfied with the arrangements,
The angels, drifting off, felt secure
In their privilege, but less good.

CLEANING LADY

She is the spirit of this house,
Matty, a dark absence of something
Without which it's impossible to love,
Eat, sleep, even die properly.

The sofa purrs when she strokes it,
The refrigerator lights up, opening
To her face, and before her the children feel
Transparent in their paleness.

She is the spirit in whose swept
Powerful consequence their daddy lives
Without knowing its name, though once
He drove her home to the dark side of the world.

And she is the genius their mommy appeases
With money, face averted, eyes
Not, as the brown palm submits
To the cool oppression of cash.

Not that Matty in her own house,
The sofa lumpy with her drugged son,
Has any witchcraft. The lamp cord
Proves her mortal, tripping her every time.

In fact, she feels something missing
In herself that she finds like disappointment
At the other house, a dangerous leisure
That she stalks warily with a feather duster.

And there's no end to dust. They know it,
She knows it, and no end to the labor of spirits
Unequal before it. But someone has to clean up
Again. Someone has to survive this leisure.

DIVISION OF LABOR

Hey! Iris, you're going to be our whore,
Manuel is going to pick all the grapes here,
Sam will sell us the squeezings Saturday night,
And Booker is going to dance for us or die.

I'm Jimmy whose dad sold the used cars
To get here. I played left halfback, attended
Law school, am your congressman, I think,
Or judge. I was appointed by a death.

Now I'm dividing the labor. Somebody said
(Maybe dad): Divide the labor. So I divide.
Somebody said: Don't put square pegs
In round holes. And then somebody died.

Don't worry. When a life won't fit, I send it
To dad who finds it a place down there for nothing.

SIXTIETH ANNUAL
ETHNOLOGICAL SURVEY

Zunis are out there chanting still
From the beginning, to bring on rain
By the right words in the right order,
And children, health, long life, to keep
The dead alive, roads open,
The future habitable, the world together.

We thank the Zunis, and ask for them
Miracle drugs and TV,
That we alone can offer who,
In isolation ward, in laboratory,
Separate out the troubling variant,
Like the chant that fails over and over.

On a map we contain the Zunis, as they
Include us in their best wishes.

THE PENANCE

This is the penance: a recurring dream,
This child running down the road, its mouth
A hole filled up with blackness, its little wings
Two flares of napalm and it runs toward you.

You can't yet hear its scream but know it's screaming,
Know if it can reach you, it will try to
Hug you and that napalm is contagious,
A deadly foreign plague for darker people.

Nothing can save you—voting, letters, marches—
So you close your eyes. A hundred years
It seems to take, the child getting nearer,
Bigger, maybe not so scared as furious.

Now you hear its scream—a supersonic
Jet-like whine that peels your skin off patch
By patch, and then the face is in your face,
Close as a lover's, eyes as bleak as bullets.

Then black-out till you wake forgetting all,
Forgetting him who felt the burning arms
Around him, but who can't, it seems, save any
Thing that matters though he knows what matters.

So this is the penance: a recurring dream
That you're awake and doing good, loving
The children, saving for their education
And your own retirement—till you close your eyes.

V

A FEW OCCASIONS

TO CELEBRATE

STONECUTTER'S HOLIDAY

> "We always do it; no one ever notices
> it, but we always create a small flaw
> in every image; it's for safety!"
>   (R. K. Narayan)

He is forcing by knock, tap, and whittle
This block into the form of a goddess
Because there is nothing better to do
And the chisel's clink is the cry of granite
Yielding itself chip by chip
As he leans into it, blowing crumbs
Of rock away from nakedness, to foin
Again, again, knowing that soon
He is going to have Her.
                        One more blow—
Ha!—for the heart that wanted once
To say "I love you" right and didn't,
One for the mind that thought there was more
To being a man than could be proved
By looking at people.
                      And when he is done
He will ask Her to speak coldly, not
Of Her poor maker, but of a form
Suitable for enduring the weather
And the wearing arms of men.
                        Then,
He will leave as his mark on Her perfection
Some little hidden flaw to make Her,
For the world's hard uses, human.

RETIREMENT PARTY

It was like committing suicide
When the tide was out, sloshing flat miles
Into the low gray sea, ankles chilled,
Sinuses filling, gulls flapping over.

This is silly. It was more like waking
From fifty-years' service as a flywheel
In a gold watch that ticked seconds
Like days in a life of less than a minute.

Star, he said to a western blue evangel,
Star, what's in it for us who move
Gravely to extinction? Should we buy dynamite?
Should we explode naked into the last asylum?

This also is silly, but he liked it,
Him and that star, twins of an elegant routine,
A superhuman habit to no end,
So time itself sang like a cricket in his fob.

TRYING

He has, by his wife's reckoning, failed so often,
He thinks failure is just trying, so the cat's
Got his daughter's love, the car his son's reverence,
And birds beat and rob him in his own garden,
Leaving him for caterpillars and aphids to peck at.

But each afternoon he raises his hose again
And out of it leaps a sweet unstinting jet
Whose shed plumes of spray, mixing with sun,
Unfurl a rainbow so dim and delicate
No one but he can see the good he's done.

HAY FEVER

In the spread kingdom of Acacia
The April air is raining gold,
Sweet particles drenching the headlands,
Boiling up the river systems
Until, gasping for breath, the world
Is seen through a waste of tears, the word
Gargled in mounting waters.
                        Surplus
Of flowering, of fluids, of being
In the swollen season, bees sunk
Under its load, smothered
By the sheer joy of making.

In this flawed system, the face blossoms,
Praising by cough, sneeze
And the misery of itch and ugly red
The nonsense of God's blind plenty,
Saying: suffer this little evil.

In such waste is
The hope of children,
The stigma and lavish proof
Of love.

HONORABLE MENTION

It's some kind of little gray-leafed
Wild flower on the wind side
Of the dune and bent by habit
Hard away from the sea.

Between the great tides
And counter tides, its minute attention
Clutches down, grasping at the favor
Of indifferent rocks.

And after all the prizes are passed out,
Its yellow bloom seems futile,
Except to bees who also make a sweetness
Out of small desperation.

SHORT PASTORAL

Three-days rain and,
Right in the middle of town
This small farmhouse.
                        I could have
Dressed, rushed out, come back
In five minutes with a wild
Armful of wet apples
Or one warm egg
For a love gift.
                  Freud
Was out in the barn
Munching hay with Marx,
And Darwin dozed in the loft.

We were alone for miles
With honest coffee
And a few words. You said:
I'd sure hate to live in town.
I said: This farming—
It won't pay.

SKINS

It's raining. I'm dry and warm. I'm full.
O sweet stove, refrigerator, lights,
Walls, curtains, toasted air,
Pajamas, my own skin, my dears.

Then this voice betrays me, my own,
Saying coldly: "You think you're at home.
You're not at home. These skins
Aren't yours, not even your own.

Shut off the gas, power, money
And you'd hump between the state hospital
And the bus station, the drape of your pants
An old man's drape, loose on the boneys."

All the more I love you, skins, because
You are not mine, unpossessable
But here nevertheless now,
Like Monique or Sarah or one I forget:

Kind to a man who pays the rent.

TO THE CITY

I am a man.
I can't sleep under a leaf.
I can't kill for food
As the spider, innocent.
I can't sing the necessity
Of being a cricket at dusk.
I can't even say the city
Was made for humans.

There, I met Raven under the streetlight.
He carried a knife and had himself
A good deal going.
I found Melanie in a bar,
Her purse full of fives
From the traffic, and Eve
In a little room with sixteen pills
Sleeping on her collapsed chest,
And the general on horseback,
A senseless stone in the park.

Maybe somewhere ahead
On parquetry floors
In sunlight, almost transparent,
Our betters are waiting.
Maybe we can't quite hear their gauzy voices
Call back: "Wake up! Wake up!
You're way overdue. There's another life yet."

Dear Melanie, Raven
My brother, tell our Eve,
If she's still with us,
How the general strokes the neck
Of his horse with a thoughtful hand.
Tell her we are the hard people.
Who find even in stone
Some gentleness.

TREES

He said there's a time when to write
About trees is a crime. I see old pine,
Old buckeye, old orange beaten back
So we can house assassins who won't write
About trees or people, but of numbers killed,
Starved, pacified, liberated.
There are some redwoods hollowed by lightning,
A family could live in. Cherry never hurt
The most politically conscious man,
Or, shading his thought, might have done him good.
I'm going to write about trees, how they vote,
Fight, what they want and believe in;
I'm going to ask apple what it is
To be human, how it feels to be one in a million.

THE GURU

Apple tree, winter apple, old ascetic,
I'm going to give up this life
And study with you.

The blossoms went. You did not live
For the blossoms. The fruit went and the leaves.
You did not live for them.

Bird beak, worm jaw, grasping hands,
And finally the wind took it all away
Leaving you out in the cold, detached.

You can sing now, make love, be charitable
With no expectation, the thing itself,
Free. What's appearance to you?

Spring, that sweet swindle for bees,
Summer, a mere green mystique,
Fall, rotting already at the core.

I'm going to sit at your feet
And listen to your long silences.
I'm going to follow breathing down to its roots.

And when spring comes, we're going to laugh
At the blossoms together.
We're going to blossom together laughing.

AUDIT

Listen. Wind hangs in the pine branches.
The year is done. There are certain things against you.
The lull is around the house, waiting.
But moss on the cold side of the bark is with you,
A jackrabbit frozen at the odor of fox is with you,
And a last apple, with a worm in it.
If you could see through the mist, a heaven of stars
And the granite under the dirt are perhaps with you.
When you close your book, its story will be with you too,
This plot of a traveler who against a sea came home,
His life his prize. If you listen minutely enough
Even the worm in the star, the fox in the rabbit's
Clenched heart are with you, though they seem hard companions.

On the north side of this thought, the moss is ready
To fend off the wind; or you breathe, and the wind is with you.

LIBRARY OF CONGRESS CATALOGING IN PUBLICATION DATA
Nathan, Leonard Edward, 1924-
  Returning your call.

  (Princeton series of contemporary poets)
  I. Title.
PS3564.A849R4   811'.5'4   75-3485
ISBN 0-691-06296-X

GPSR Authorized Representative: Easy Access System Europe - Mustamäe tee 50, 10621 Tallinn, Estonia, gpsr.requests@easproject.com

www.ingramcontent.com/pod-product-compliance
Lightning Source LLC
Chambersburg PA
CBHW071934240426
43668CB00038B/1795